PRAISE FOR LIFE AFTER THE SILENCE

"Angela shares some dynamic principles of the grace and love of God towards his children. These principles highlights how one's life can be redefined by unfortunate circumstances to reinvigorate one's life. Thus, her story becomes an agent of change for others who desire to seek emotional and spiritual restoration."

-Nicole Barber, LCPC

"Hope, sacrifice, and determination enter my spirit when I read excerpts from this book. Angela's story is traumatic and anyone who experienced what she did could have stayed in the bed under the covers with the curtains drawn. However, Angela is GOD's chosen Angel, and her name alone says so, "Angela.

She is a warrior who has overcome the unthinkable and unimaginable. I hope that Angela knows how inspirational her experience and work is to other's who have had similar experiences."

-Dr. Kimberly Y. Johnson

Shonda,

You are Amazing!
Thank you for your
love & Support.

In Power & Purpose!

♡ Angela

♡

LIFE
AFTER
THE SILENCE

FROM PAIN TO POWER TO PURPOSE

ANGELA D. WHARTON

ANGELA D.
WHARTON
INTERNATIONAL

LIFE AFTER THE SILENCE
Copyright © 2015 by Angela D. Wharton

Unless otherwise indicated, scripture quotations are from the *Holy Bible: New International Version*®, (North American Edition). Copyright © 1973, 1978, 1984 by International Bible Society. All rights reserved.

Editor: Brian Reinthaler Editing
Cover Designer: Emanuel Brown Design
Interior Design: Purposely Created Publishing

Printed in the United States of America

First trade paperback printing, 2015

ISBN: 978-0-692-36074-3

Angela D. Wharton International
PO Box 24774
Middle River, MD 21220-3975
angeladwharton@gmail.com
(443) 317-3070

This book is dedicated to my two precious little angels who were extremely patient with mommy throughout this process.

■ ■ ■

And to my husband, for always believing in me and loving me through some of my toughest moments.

■ ■ ■

And to all who have and are suffering in silence from the pain of sexual violence.

TABLE OF CONTENTS

FOREWORD

It would be innocuous of me to report that in a culture of hyper sexualized movies, music and television that sexual acts against women, men and children are non-existent. Unfortunately, jarring statistics report that one in every four women will be sexually assaulted and one in every six men will report the same. But as sobering as the statics are, I'm thankful of the vision and strength that the author shares in *Life After the Silence: From Pain, to Power, to Purpose.* Delicately, with love and passion, this book counsels victims of sexual assault, while inserting theological principals undergirding how God's grace can heal and restore.

Helping one move from destruction to redemption is a skill that can't be taught but only manifested through one's own unique experience. *Life After the Silence: From Pain, to Power, to Purpose* not only deals with the victim's physical pains but how he or she can grow psychological, emotionally and spiritually. I'm thankful that God has equipped my daughter in Christ to be the vessel to birth this phenomenal book of healing and transformation.

Dr. Jamal-Harrison Bryant

Pastor, Author, Philanthropist

INTRODUCTION

For years, sexual violence has been prevalent in our communities and, far too often, society has often turned a blind eye. No one wanted to hear about, let alone talk about it. The lesson we tacitly received was that this is something that should never be discussed. Such thinking produces a community of Survivors who suffer in silence—afraid to speak up which is especially tragic because giving voice to the pain is one of the first steps in the healing process.

Are you tired of suffering in silence? Are you fed up with blaming yourself for the sexual assault or abuse that you have been subjected to? Do you wrestle with fear? Are you losing that fight? Are you ready to overcome the persistent obstacles that stifle your progress? Are you willing to take action in order to move forward? If so, then this book is for you.

I have overcome the pain of sexual violence, psychological abuse, abandonment, depression, suicidal thoughts, and unhealthy relationships and transformed these experiences into the fuel that drives me to change the world. In the pages that follow, you will witness how I refused to give in to the negative, self-defeating chatter in my mind and how I broke free of the bondage of silence. You will share in my journey to the realization that the sexual violence I suffered was not my fault. You will learn how to take action despite the presence of fear.

I have come to know God as a healer and deliverer, and I invite you to embrace the life lessons present in the bible scriptures in this book. I am confident that they will bare the purpose in both your pain and Life After the Silence.

I wrote this book because you need to know that you are not alone and that God can move you from a place of darkness and depression into a place of light and love. You need to know and understand that there is value in your voice. Not only does it allow you to break free from suffering in silence, but also allows you to take back your power from those who have hurt you. Reading this book will empower you to conquer your fears, take hold of the hope and healing that lies before you and turn your pain into power.

Angela

· 1 ·

THE SILENCED VOICE

Aw man, I gotta go to Aunt Judy's house again?
I overheard Mom on the telephone talking to her best friend Reese.

"Chile, I gotta work the graveyard shift again tonight—they workin' me like a Hebrew slave. I'm so tired, but I need the money or we gon' be set out."

"But Mommy," I interrupted, "I don't want to go. Tony and Kandy don't want me there anyway, they say I get on their nerves. Besides, they ain't got no food anyway and I'm tired of eating fried baloney and jelly at their house. I want some real food and I want it in my own house."

My mom worked long hours day and night, and since it was just the two of us at home, she usually had to leave me with Aunt Judy and my teenaged cousins Tony and Kandy. I was like the annoying little sister they could not get rid of—like a piece of bubble gum on the bottom of their shoes.

■ ■ ■

"I had such a great day at school!" I told my big cousins as they walked me home on that warm May day.

Tony and Kandy, who were about 13 and 15 at the time, were uninterested. They were mad to be stuck picking me up when they could have been playing double-dutch or skillet with their friends. I went on anyway.

"Hey y'all, guess what? Mrs. Smith said that my behavior was exemplary!" I proudly enunciated each syllable of the compliment my teacher had given. "Yeah, my behavior was exemplary, and if you don't know, it means I was the best of the best—I set the example of what excellent behavior should be."

As a child, I loved words, especially unusual ones I didn't hear often at home. I read the dictionary on a daily basis and often experimented in conversation with words I had recently learned.

"Exemplary?" Kandy scowled. "Why you gotta always be using big words? Don't nobody know what that means and don't nobody care. You always think you better than everybody else 'cause you be using them big words. You ain't all that, you ain't that smart."

I felt instantly deflated, as if crushed under my cousin's foot like a soda can. And thus began the self-admonishing chatter in my head.

Maybe I do think I'm better than them. I should stop using big words. It's not polite to make them feel "less than."

I remember this like it was yesterday. I had been silenced. And my love for words had been trampled. From that moment, I stopped reading my dictionary, I learned to avoid experimenting in conversation and I took extra pains to avoid using big words, not only with my cousins, but with everyone, all at the expense of my own happiness, my own growth and my own intelligence. I was 7 years old.

What happened to my voice? Why did I allow them to make me feel "less than"? Why did I allow my voice to be stolen?

What I now know is that their criticism of me was their issue, not mine. Perhaps Tony and Kandy saw in me what they wanted to be, but were not. Perhaps this is what led them to demean me. Regardless, I accepted it as my truth.

We are not taught as children that we ought not let others' opinions of us define who we are. Indeed, we are encouraged to mind our manners, respect our elders, please our teachers and avoid hurting others' feelings. But this sensitivity also leads to absorbing others' opinions of us, internalizing them and allowing them to govern our lives well into our adulthood. When this behavior is not addressed, it turns into what I call "shrinkage" — when you "shrink" or diminish yourself so as not to shine brighter than others, and so as to protect their feelings or insecurities at the expense of your own.

But Matthew 5:16 says, "Let your light shine before others, so that they may see your good works and give glory to your Father who is in heaven."

We must stand up, speak up and let our voices be heard. Suffering in silence is no longer an option.

"Never be bullied into silence. Never allow yourself to be made a victim. Accept no one's definition of your life. Define yourself." –Robert Frost

· 2 ·

THE THINGS WE DON'T TALK ABOUT

Letter to my mother, dated July 3, 2012:

Mommy, it saddens me to have to tell you this and I apologize for holding it in for so long but... Do you remember that guy you dated when we lived on Eager Street? He was from your past and was just out of the service and you met back up with him? I don't remember his name but I do remember he was dark skinned and wore a military jacket.

Well, he called the house one night just as Sedra had finished my hair and said he wanted to come over and talk to me. I told him you were not home and that there was no reason for him to come over. He insisted. He said he just wanted to talk to me about how I could make money to help you. So I finally said okay and hung up. I begged Sedra not to leave me because something just didn't feel right, but she said she had to go because it was 9:30pm and she was already in trouble. He got there after she left. He wanted to stay in the living room to talk, which I thought was strange because it was always dark in there, but I said okay. He told me I could make a lot of money as a phone sex operator. All I had to do is talk to men that called and get paid. I kept telling him no and asked him to leave, but he wouldn't stop. He made me feel guilty about helping you with bills and stuff. I don't know if you told him we were poor, but he knew that we didn't have much money. He kept saying, "Don't you want to help your mom? You know she works really hard to provide for you and your brother? Don't you want to buy yourself some Jordache jeans like the rest of your little girlfriends wear?"

I finally gave in. He then said he needed a sample. I said, "A sample? What do you mean?" He said he needed a sample of me to take to his boss so he could decide if I was right for the job. He said we should go downstairs to my room. I said no and told him to leave. But he wouldn't. He started making me feel guilty again, so I said okay. We got downstairs to my room and he immediately took off his pants and underwear and got in my bed. I was really nervous and scared now, but I got in with all of my clothes still on. He rolled over on top of me and I started to fight him off of me. I fought as he tried to get my pants off, ripping the buttons. I kept saying, "No! Stop!" but he wouldn't.

He proceeded to enter me. And I said, "If you don't stop I'll scream rape!" He jumped up and said, "How you 'gon call this rape when you let me in? You let me down here to you room!" Lying there in absolute fear, I never said a word.

All of sudden, the doorbell rang! I grabbed my pants and pulled them on, running upstairs to answer the door. It was Phil. Your boyfriend was already dressed and right behind me as I let Phil in. He said "Whassup?" to Phil and

"See you later!" to me, and was gone. Right away, Phil asked me what was wrong and I told him I was just tired. He raised his voice a bit and said, "No, what's wrong with you?" And I repeated that I was just tired. I went upstairs and he followed me. I got a safety pin, pinned my pants together and got in your bed with Toye. Phil got in too and watched TV. I fell asleep and to this day, I don't remember what happened after that.

I do remember one day, some time after this, you and I were in the kitchen talking and I said, "Ma, remember that guy you used to see from the service?" You said, "Yeah?" and I said, "I don't like him..."

The sexual assault I described in this letter had taken place almost 26 years earlier, in the Fall of 1986, when I was just 14 years old.

At age 24, I was faced with the harsh reality of sexual assault yet again. It was Friday, November 22, 1996. In those days, I normally would go out on the town with my friends, but that particular Friday evening I decided to go home and curl up with my books and get some homework done. I returned home from getting my hair done at my friend Nicole's house earlier than expected. I gathered my purse, got out of the car and walked up the dimly lit path toward my apartment building with my head down, mentally scheduling my night. A few of the street lights had been blown, which made it even darker. As I lifted my head to reach for the doorknob, I noticed a man standing to the left of me pulling a mask over his head.

He held a handgun, pointed it straight at me, and said, "Give me your purse and turn around and walk that way." He directed me to the back of the apartment building, and I began to silently recite the 23rd Psalm. The Lord is my shepherd, I shall not want...

As we continued to walk through the woods, he began blurting out all kinds of obscenities and I continued to pray to God to help me. We finally got to a clearing of grass and he walked from behind me, stood in front of me, and leveled the barrel of the gun on my forehead. The touch of cold steel sent chills throughout my body and I began frantically pleading for my life. He told me to shut the f@%& up and get down on my knees. I was forced to perform orally on him as he held the handgun to my left temple. After some time, he forced me down on the ground.

I thought to myself as I lay there on the cold, crisp, dew-dampened grass, "My, look at all the stars out in the sky tonight. How beautiful they are...but where's the moon?" It was all I could do to take my mind off of what was about to happen to me. I remember the cold ache of the gun jabbing into the left side of my stomach as he violently took what belonged to me, the most private part of me...

For a moment, I felt nothing; I went numb as he continued to push into me. It was like I was in limbo; neither here nor there. I remember silently praying, God, please help me.

And then, something happened.

It was as if God had taken my spirit out of my body and brought it up with Him. I was having an out-of-body experience; out of my body and into God's presence! I knew my body was lying on the grass being brutally assaulted at gunpoint by this crazed person, but I had an aerial view of the horrible event. I could see everything as if God had taken me up to sit with Him. Hallelujah! It was as if God wanted to be sure that my spirit was not harmed in any way, shape or form. And although my body was harmed, my spirit was not.

Events like these shake us to our core. And too often we do not talk about them. There is an old saying in our community that goes "What happens in our house, stays in our house." You do not tell the family's business. But there are hundreds of thousands of us who have been sexually assaulted or abused, including many as children. Many of us have grown into adults who carry on with our daily lives, all the while suffering in silence. We try to bury this awful thing that has happened to us, this act that has stolen our innocence and stifled our childhood or even our growth as adults.

Making matters worse, Survivors of sexual violence often attempt to "self-medicate." They try to ease the pain by engaging in sexual promiscuity, drug and alcohol abuse or other self-destructive behaviors. According to RAINN.org, Survivors of sexual violence are 13 times more likely to abuse alcohol and 26 times more likely to abuse drugs. Self-medication never works; it only perpetuates the issues. You must take the time to do the work required to heal.

> **"She believed she could heal...and she did."**
>
> *–Angela D. Wharton*

. 3 .

FINDING MY VOICE

I just wanted to take a bath. I wanted to wash off the dirt, twigs, leaves, bugs, guilt, shame, blame, fear, pain... I wanted to wash HIM off of me! I needed to feel normal again; to be cleansed of this awful violation of my body.

My mom ran a bath. "Come on baby it's time to get in."

Although I so desperately wanted to take a bath, I could not bring myself to take off my brother's t-shirt, pants and socks. I had been given his clothes to wear after detectives demanded each piece of my clothing to check for evidence of the crime committed.

"It's okay if you are not ready yet," Mom said. "Take your time, baby."

She left the room and I sat on that toilet seat for what felt like forever. Finally, I took a deep breath, undressed and got in. The water was warm and I eased in and sat down. I could feel sting of the water on my fresh open wounds. The searing pain brought back vivid images of what had taken place just hours earlier and I began to scream at the top of my lungs and shake uncontrollably.

Mom sprinted back to the bathroom, grabbed me and held me tight.

"I'm here baby, no one can hurt you now," she said. "He can't hurt you now, you are safe here with me."

But I could not stop. There were no words, just screams. Those screams were coming from a place of pain—emotional and physical. After some time, my mom finally was able to calm me enough to get me gently washed up and out of the tub. Although my body was clean, my mind still felt tainted with rape. I felt like I would never be clean again.

"Close the blinds and the curtains, Mom!" I cried out as I laid in the middle of Mom's bed, careful not to get near either edge. "He might see me."

His final words to me had been, "You bet' not scream, tell anyone or go to the police. I know where you live and I know what kind of car you drive—I will find you and I will kill you."

I believed he was going to kill me. I had done everything he told me not to, so I was as good as dead. I just knew that he was on the roof across the street, waiting for a clear shot. This time, he would kill me.

I pulled the comforter up to my neck and prayed, but images of the woods, the mask, and the gun kept playing in my head as I tried to fall asleep. I just wanted them to go away. So I prayed anew, Lord, please take the pain and fear away so that I may rest—you are the only one who can do it. In Jesus' name, Amen.

I finally fell asleep, only to be awakened by the fear that he had found me, and I began to scream and shake uncontrollably yet again. No words—just blood curdling screams. This continued for some time.

The nights that followed were filled with insomnia, nightmares and periods of screaming in horror. The trauma of being sexually violated made it impossible for my brain to form words amidst these nighttime terrors. I eventually sought the help of a therapist, who worked with me for more than two years. A combination of prayer and therapy helped me heal.

■ ■ ■

A couple years later, I ran into my old neighbor from the apartment below where I had been living the night I was raped. I had not returned since. My family had pulled together the next morning and moved all of my stuff into Mom's house to spare me the pain of having to revisit the scene.

He was excited to see me because he did not know what had happened to me. He had heard that I was raped, but did not want not believe it, so I attempted to tell him.

Immediately, I felt a nauseating pain in the pit of my stomach. As I began to speak, I became terribly lightheaded and vomited right on the sidewalk. It was as if my mouth was a faucet he had just turned on. Shocked by my physical reaction, he apologized repeatedly. Through tears of embarrassment, I returned his apologies and said I had to go. As I ran off, I could still hear him apologizing in the distance. I never got the chance to even speak the words; my body simply shut down my attempt to recall the event in my mind.

For years after this, I was unable to speak my story without becoming physically ill. So I did not. I knew at the time that many people, including family members, were aware of what had happened to me, but they did not speak of it either; at least not in front of me. Have you ever felt that awkward moment when you walk into the room and all of a sudden, everyone stops talking and you instantly know that you were the topic of discussion? I experienced that on many occasions.

It was not until another 5 years had passed, when I had the opportunity to describe the events to a close friend, that I was able to find my voice. I had gotten to the point where I could no longer hold it in, or remain silent—I had to break free of the bondage of silence. I felt like I could not breathe and that opening my mouth to speak my truth was the only way to get air. My friend provided that safe space for me and I was and I was finally able to make it through the entire story without a barf bag or a trash can.

Telling my story in detail without becoming sick or breaking down in tears was a momentous accomplishment. It represented a new milestone in my healing process and set me on the path to turning this awful chapter in my life into something from which I (and others) might draw strength.

Breaking the silence and speaking up and out about my story was a critical step in the process of healing the wounds I had suffered from sexual violence. Once I was able to get below the surface and share the painful details of my story, a tremendous load was lifted from my shoulders. I could finally breathe, as though free from bondage. And I decided, from that day forward, I would no longer live in silence.

I was no longer afraid to proclaim that I am a Survivor of sexual violence. The imaginary, flashing neon sign that read, "I was raped" no longer hung around my neck. I shared my story with friends, family, colleagues, and strangers in the grocery store—with whomever I could when circumstances permitted. And I felt good about it. I was not ashamed. It was as if someone had flipped on the switch to my voice. And I have since come to realize that only I have the power to turn it off.

Of course, that will never happen. Events in the years that followed left me with no doubt that I am on assignment from God to give Survivors hope in the face of hopelessness, courage in the presence of fear, and strength to break their silence and move to forgiveness. Only you have the power to find your voice. I found mine in speaking my truth, in illuminating the darkness in my life, and now I have made a career of speaking to others. Perhaps your voice is in poetry, art, singing, fashion design—whatever it is, I urge you to begin the journey to find it and use it sooner rather than later.

. 4 .

UNCOVERING THE TRUTH

In April 2003, I received an invite from my good friend and co-worker, Netta, to attend Morning Star Baptist Church's Good Friday service, which was being held that morning at the Baltimore Convention Center.

I love attending Good Friday services, as they mark the day of my Lord and Savior Jesus Christ's death on the cross so that we may have a right to the Tree of Life. Hearing my Savior's seven last words preached reminds me of the greatest sacrifice that anyone has ever made for me.

"Okay, Netta," I said. "I'll meet you out front of the Convention Center."

I hung up the phone, got into my car and drove downtown. As it began to rain, I realized that I did not have an umbrella, so I stopped by my mother's house to borrow one. By the time I was back in my car, the rain was falling like you would not believe. It was as if the sky had just opened up.

The pit stop at Mom's, along with the torrential downpour, already had me running late, so the MTA bus clogging up traffic in my lane worked my last nerve.

"Oh my gosh, come on bus!" I complained. "Can you go any slower? I am going to be late! COME! ON!"

Fed up, I put on my left signal and attempted to pass. Of course, as I drew even with the bus, the driver sped up, and I could not get in front of him. Out of the corner of my eye, a blue mini-van came careening from my left.

"Jesus!" I screamed and felt my entire body stiffen as it prepared for impact.

I saw nothing but white.

God? Jesus? Am I dead?

What seemed like an eternity of silence passed before, suddenly, I heard a man's voice calling frantically to me, "Ma'am? Ma'am, are you okay?"

"No, I'm hurt."

He said his name was Nate and that the ambulance would be here very soon. He told me that he would stay with me until the paramedics arrived.

"Sir, please call my mom and tell her what happened," I pleaded. "I just left her."

Nate found my phone on the floor of my now mangled gold and white Jeep Cherokee and called my mom. He told her that I would be transported to nearby Johns Hopkins Hospital.

The paramedics asked me a bunch of questions upon their arrival, and I recall not being able to answer many of them. I did tell someone that I needed to get to church—I just wanted to get to Good Friday service. I felt searing pain in my legs as they put me on a stretcher and rolled me to the ambulance.

Once inside and stabilized, I asked one of paramedics to call Netta. She did and put the phone to my ear.

"Netta, I won't be able to meet you," I mumbled. "I just had an accident and am in the ambulance."

"What?!" I remember the shock in her voice. "Oh my God, okay, I will check on you later."

On the way to the hospital, I prayed, "Don't let me die now, God. It's not time yet." I knew full well that I had not yet done what He had called me to do.

My mom and family members were already at the hospital when I arrived, and my aunt exclaimed, "Here she is!"

Tears rolled down my mother's face as she swiftly accompanied my stretcher down the hall to the emergency room.

"My baby, are you okay?"

I could not muster the strength to answer. oI underwent a series of tests and x-rays to evaluate the extent of my injuries. Hours later, the doctor returned to the Emergency Room to inform me of his amazement that I had suffered no broken bones, ruptures or internal bleeding; all of my tests were negative. He said that I should consider myself blessed.

Of course, he was preaching to the choir. I am more than blessed; I am a child of God. Isaiah 54:17 says, "No weapon formed against you shall prosper, and every tongue that rises against you in judgment, you shall condemn." That car accident was a weapon formed by Satan to try to devour me, but it did not prosper. Glory to God for He showed me that miracles do happen.

Days later, I was informed that my Jeep had been totaled. I visited the Baltimore City Impound to get all of my personal items out of it. I was escorted in a sedan down a winding road of abandoned and junked cars to the very end of the road. The driver called my name and tag number.

"Yes, but that's not my Jeep," I answered.

He read my name and tag number again, adding, "Ma'am, this is your vehicle. Kindly gather your personal items. I'll wait for you."

I got out of the sedan and stood in front of the jeep, awestruck. I began to weep and cry out to God, thanking Him for saving my life. The damage to my vehicle was a clear reminder that I am to remain here on this side of Heaven just a little while longer.

I had a difficult time recovering from these traumatic events. It was not until I heard Pastor Joel Osteen say that we must change our perspective that I understood that God allows each test, trial and tribulation to take place in our lives in an effort to prepare us for our next level. Pastor Osteen mentioned that, once we realize that these things are not happening to us, but for us, we can begin to understand Romans 8:28, which states, "And we know that all things work together for good to them that love God, to them who are the called according to his purpose."

. 5 .

THE POWER WITHIN YOU

"I can't believe we're going on a cruise!"

I cried out with joy as I danced around our bedroom, holding up a one-piece bathing suit that I had been waiting for the perfect time to wear. What better opportunity than the Caribbean cruise my husband, Darnyle, had surprised me with to celebrate our fourth wedding anniversary with our friends, Mike and Tina.

I had always wanted to go on a cruise—the people in the commercials always looked like they were having the time of their lives. And for the first part of our September 2009 trip, so did we. We attended shows, shopped and partied like crazy. Oh, and the food! Twenty-four hours a day!

On the day before we were scheduled to arrive in the Bahamas, we signed up as a group for the Snorkeling and Beach Adventure. Though I could not swim, I figured I would be okay to snorkel with a life preserver, so we got off our Carnival cruise ship, boarded a catamaran with about 30 other adventurers, and set off into the sea.

The captain soon found what he thought was the ideal spot for snorkeling and attempted to drop the anchor. After a minute, a loud grinding noise began emanating from beneath the boat. And then, silence. Twice more the captain tried to lower the anchor to no avail. The man sitting next to my husband explained that the waters were too rough to secure the anchor.

We sailed on for another ten minutes before stopping again, but still the anchor would not catch. I began to wonder if maybe this trip was not such a good idea.

God, why did I come on this excursion? I prayed as I looked out over the churning water. I can't swim and feel very scared right now, please grant me your peace and comfort.

On the third try, we finally were able to anchor the catamaran and, before long, Mike, Tina and Darnyle had all jumped in to swim and snorkel. I sat on the boat with all of my gear on and, as I contemplated whether or not I should get in, one of the crew members jumped in a speedboat and zoomed out to rescue a man who had been carried a few hundred yards away in the strong current.

Shortly thereafter, a young lady climbed back onto the catamaran and warned, "If I were you, I would not go in. The waters are too choppy."

Despite my better instincts, I did not want to be left out of the fun. I just smiled and decided to get in line to snorkel. As I waited, I prayed to God for a word or indication to confirm my decision. As I arrived at the front of the line and reached out to the crew member to help me into the water, the captain called out for his assistance.

"Miss, please wait until I return," the crewman instructed. "Do not get in without my help."

I took that as my sign from God not to get into the water. I turned right around, went back to my seat and took off all of my gear.

Eventually everyone was called back to the catamaran so that we could move on to the beach tour part of our excursion and we began sailing to Zanzibar Beach, which was not far from our snorkeling location. We were met about a quarter of a mile off the beautiful beach by a speed boat. As we prepared to exit the catamaran, Tina grabbed me.

"Angela, put your life jacket on," she said. "We don't want anything to happen to you."

"Oh yeah, thanks girl," I answered and quickly strapped on the safety vest.

The speed boat carried about eight of us over to the beach. Once there, we found the perfect spot on the sand to feel the waves crashing onto the shore and just relaxed for a while before heading to the Zanzibar Café to grab some lunch.

After lunch, the guys did a little beach snorkeling while Tina and I splashed around close to the shore, but before long the crew was calling out to us to get ready to leave. A few people from our group were already getting on the pontoon to be transported back to the catamaran.

We had decided to hang back a little longer so that we could be the last ones to go, but the captain, apparently way behind schedule, called urgently for everyone left on the beach to board the pontoon immediately. I did not have time to put my safety vest back on and, as we got on the speed boat, everyone was urged to hurry and give their vests to the captain. I reluctantly handed mine over and watched him place it on the floor under his seat. Immediately, I felt an uneasiness in my stomach that I could not shake.

The boat took off at top speed, crashing against the waves and carrying at least ten more people than it had when we landed on the beach. We were packed on like sardines in a can. Tina and I clung to the poles that secured the awning of the pontoon, while Darnyle and Mike did the same directly across from us.

Halfway out to the catamaran, the crewman working the back of our boat called out,

"Yo, we are taking in too much water in the back! Everyone, move to the front!"

We all scooted forward, step-by-itty-bitty-step, as the boat heaved treacherously from side to side, crashing down on one wave after another. I shrieked aloud with each sway of the pontoon and vivid thoughts of overturning flooded my brain. My stomach was in knots and my body stiffened with fear as I imagined myself drowning.

"Bae, look at me," Darnyle said, desperately trying to shift my attention to him from across the boat as it quickly approached the catamaran. Our eyes met. "We are not going to flip over."

But just as the words left his lips, the boat rocked and I felt my back crash against the ocean. The boat had flipped, sending everyone on board and all of our belongings into the frothing sea.

As I sunk deeper into the crystal clear water, I could see the sky shrinking away from above me, and again, I began to pray.

God don't let me die like this, please. My baby Asia needs me—I can't die now, I'm not done yet.

Just then, I was filled with a strength that I did not know I had and began to push and fight toward the beautiful blue sky. I had to make it back above the water; I could not leave my baby girl in the world without her mommy. I fought and fought, reaching higher and higher until I resurfaced.

As my head emerged, I screamed for help at the top of my lungs. All I could hear was Darnyle's panicked voice shouting in desperation. He thought that I had drowned when he did not see me immediately.

"Yo, where's my wife?! Where's my wife?!"

I had surfaced just inches from the overturned boat and the gritty barnacles on its underside sliced painfully through my left arm as I tried to hang on for dear life.

"God, please help me," I cried, as my husband swam toward me.

Finally, someone threw the life ring from the catamaran and pulled us to the safety of the larger boat.

■ ■ ■

There will always be adversity in our lives; and as I noted earlier, it only shows up to make us stronger. God gave us all the personal strength and inner power we need to pull ourselves up by our four-inch heels (or bootstraps, whatever works for you) and get back in the race.

Although I initially felt helpless as I sank deeper and deeper into those Caribbean waters, I took a moment to access the power within me. In a split second, I had to look deep inside myself and decide that I would live, not die. I did not want my baby girl to endure the pain of losing her one and only mother, so I decided then and there to fight for my life. I would not be defeated.

. 6 .

BEING THE SHE-RO

"Ahhhh, everyone's medicated and asleep," I said to myself as I closed the door to my baby girl's room.

Despite my husband and two daughters suffering from horrible colds, I was quite well and decided to take a few moments to veg out on the couch. I flipped on the Trinity Broadcasting Network to find Steve Harvey hosting a show with singer and actor Tyrese Gibson as a guest. Tyrese was talking about his new book, How To Get Out of Your Own Way.

Have you ever listened to someone speaking to an audience and found that it was like they were speaking directly to you? That is how I felt listening to Tyrese. He said, "It is time to get out of your own way and do what God has called you to do." These words resonated so much that it felt like God was using Tyrese as a vehicle to get an important word directly to me. And the message was clear.

I stood up from the couch and began to walk toward the television. All of a sudden, I found myself laying prostrate on the floor before God, crying and begging to be forgiven. When I say I was crying, I mean ugly crying—snot running, face completely drenched with tears. I wanted forgiveness for not carrying out the purpose and vision for Phynyx Ministries (the nonprofit organization I founded that serves women Survivors of sexual assault) when God had given it to me fifteen years earlier.

I was physically shaken and I remember saying, "Here I am Lord. I am so sorry, please forgive me for not doing Phynyx Ministries, but I'm ready now. Yes, Lord, yes, Lord!"

In that moment, I answered the call of Phynyx Ministries. Who would have thought that God would use Steve Harvey and Tyrese Gibson as vehicles for His reminder to me to start a ministry that would change so many lives?

I knew right away that I needed my Phynyx Ministries notes—the notes I had taken while on my knees in prayer back in 1996 when God first gave me the vision. With my nose still running and tears still flowing, I tore apart my home office, living room and dining room searching for these notes, but no luck. I could not find them.

I had always kept them. No matter where I moved, I never threw them out as the years went on. I had known, deep down, that I would eventually put Phynyx Ministries into action. I just did not know when.

As I frantically restarted my search in the home office, I heard the still small voice of the Lord say, "Write it again."

"Huh?"

"Write it again," He said. "You know what I told you. Write it again."

That moment, I reached over to my desk and picked up a journal that I had received at a women's church conference in 2006. I took a deep breath, dried my face, and prepared to re-write the entire vision all over again.

Now that I had answered the call, I felt I had to tell somebody, and my brother, Leonard, was the person who came to mind. He had been only fourteen years old when I was sexually assaulted the second time and had not quite understood. But I had shared my vision of Phynyx Ministries with him a few years later, and from that point forward, he was often privy to my conversations regarding the ministry. I had regularly confided in him about wanting to start and about my fear and uncertainty on where to begin.

Journal in hand, I dialed Leonard's number. When he heard my wonderful news, he shared with me how proud he was that I had accepted the call and he vowed to support me in whatever capacity I needed. I hung up the phone and returned to the couch re-energized. I stayed up until well past midnight writing out each detail of the vision, as clearly as God had shown me back in 1996.

"And the LORD answered me, and said, Write the vision, and make it plain upon tables, that he may run that readeth it."

— Habakkuk 2:2

I wrote it and now I am running with it.

Phynyx Ministries is a Christian-based non-profit organization that provides a pathway to healing for women Survivors of sexual assault through love, support, advocacy, empowerment and education. We are a sisterhood of Survivors that provides a safe space for women to break their silence about sexual violence and move toward healing.

Many Survivors have found that, in order to heal, it is critical to share their story with someone they trust; to share that they had been sexually violated. Breaking your silence is one of the first steps in the healing process. Of course, it is not easy—no one wants to re-experience the pain of what has happened, so we often bury it as deep as we can in the hope that it will go away. But you cannot fix what you will not face. In this process, you must feel it and deal with it in order to heal from it—feel, deal and heal. I once heard someone say, "I want to inspire people. I want someone to look at me and say, 'Because of you, I did not give up.'" This is exactly how I felt upon re-writing the vision for Phynyx Ministries. I decided to take action and speak up and out for those who are still suffering in silence. I decided to share my story in an effort to change someone else's. I wanted to be the face of hope to someone—anyone—who is suffering in silence and living in darkness as a result of sexual assault. In doing so, I have begun to understand the healing power of my testimony. Now, every time I share my story, I grow stronger and the testimony becomes easier to share. My testimony and advocacy for others has, in this way, become my therapy.

But please understand that healing from sexual violence is a process. I often explain that when you are sexually assaulted/violated, it is like you are left carrying around a huge boulder—a burden so big that you can barely get your arms around it and so heavy that it literally weighs you down. But as time passes and you walk in your healing, that boulder shrinks. It becomes smaller and smaller until one day, you realize that it has become a tiny pebble that fits in your back pocket. The effects of sexual violence are always there; you simply get to a point where you realize that it no longer controls you—you control it.

When something bad happens, we have three choices. We can let it define us, let it destroy us or use it to strengthen us. Which will you choose?

· 7 ·

FACING YOUR PAST TO
CREATE YOUR FUTURE

My journey from a place of darkness and despair to one
of light and hope has not been easy. And still, I have had
good days and bad days. I have faced numerous
challenges —depression, thoughts of suicide, low self-
esteem, paranoia, unhealthy relationships, promiscuity
and feelings of unworthiness and abandonment, to
name just a few.

Overcoming such challenges is a process, part of which
involves coming to terms with different aspects of our
lives. For me, reconciling with my past was a crucial part
of this journey. It was critical to acknowledge all of the
things that were eating me up inside and driving my
poor choices, including the remnants of my two
experiences with sexual assault.

I grew up without my father. He and my mother were
teenagers when I was born and never married. My dad
married another woman and raised a family only
minutes from where we lived, but we almost never spent
time together. I was not sure why he did not visit. The
only certainty I felt was the pain from his absence. He

never picked me up from school like my classmates' fathers and never attended my school plays or other special events.

My dad was unavailable when I had my heart broken for the first time. I was only twelve at the time and I needed to ask him why that dumb boy would do that to me? I needed him to show me how a lady is to be treated and respected. I needed to feel his love so that I would not go searching for it in so many others.

I often asked myself, *why doesn't my dad want me? What is so bad about me that my own father wants nothing to do with me?* I wondered what it would be like to live in a nice house like his, to eat well like his other kids, to go shopping for name brand clothes and get warm hugs like they got.

The first time my dad visited me (after almost twenty years) was when I was raped at the age of 24, and from that point on, he never missed a birthday or Christmas. So just before my thirtieth birthday, I invited my father over to tell him exactly what I had felt all those years without him. I figured I would commemorate a milestone birthday with something big, something I had never done before. I hoped that after I had poured my heart out, he would embrace me. That I would finally get that warm hug I had so longed for and that we would live happily ever after.

It was not to be.

After emptying nearly three decades of pain and abandonment from every corner of my being, I waited in anticipation. He was silent. Nothing.

When he finally mustered up the words to speak, he told that I had turned out better growing up without him than I would have with him around.

I was blown away. Despite all that I had been through and the many mistakes I had made along the way, my dad was proud of me; proud of the woman that I had become without him. But as nice as this was to hear, his message rang hollow in my heart.

■ ■ ■

As Survivors, we do not want to feel the pain of our assaults again. We do not want to be reminded of it in any way, so we do our best to forget, to act as if it never even happened. The irony is that, to aid in these efforts, we often turn to destructive behaviors—self-medication, drug and alcohol abuse, unhealthy relationships or even promiscuity. We desperately hope that these things will soothe us and chase away the unwelcome memory. But they never do, at least not for long. The pain always returns, rearing its ugly head in some way, shape or form, and we are thrust right back into that dark place.

My struggle never involved drugs or alcohol. I was what some may call promiscuous and my relationship choices were not ideal, but I did not understand why I acted this way. I was verbally, psychologically, and emotionally abused. I was taken advantage of and disrespected. Even when the guy was great, his circumstances and/or baggage were just unhealthy. I made excuses for each guy. I believed that no one else would love me. And so, time and time again, just when I thought I should leave, I stayed. My future seemed dim.

I became entangled in an endless cycle of dating the same guy, but with a different name. Although each relationship screamed "unhealthy," I could not see or hear it and I continued to bear the psychological and emotional abuse. Why would I knowingly accept the disrespect of being humiliated in public or being a "side-chick" for years? Because my self-worth was so low that I did not feel that I deserved better.

But eventually I began to do a bit of self-reflection. I realized that I could not do this anymore. I had become physically and emotionally drained and I was spiraling out of control. I had to make a decision. I prayed morning and night for months on end, asking God him to put me in position to receive my King—the Man of God that He has for me. During this time, there was a terrible storm that blew the roof off of my home, after which the City of Baltimore declared the house condemned. I quickly had to grab a few personal items and clothing before leaving the premises.

The extended stay hotel in which I was forced to live for months after the storm was where I met the man of my dreams, the love of my life, my husband, Darnyle. He was everything that I prayed to God for. I had hit the jackpot!

Darnyle showed me what real love is. He never disrespected me and always treated me like the Queen that I am. Darnyle and I were married on the third anniversary of the day we met and on September 3, 2015 we will celebrate 10 years of marital bliss.

As a Christian woman, I had never stopped praying. Every day and night, I prayed that God would renew my mind and these prayers were the first step in my healing. Romans 12:2 says, "And do not be conformed to this world, but be transformed by the renewing of your mind, that you may prove what is that good and acceptable and perfect will of God." God changed my mind and, therefore, my perspective. I grew tired of living as I had been. I needed a transformation, and quick. I began to make some changes and created a new future for myself.

The second thing I did was forgive. Forgiveness aids in the healing process. I once read that forgiveness is not for others, but for us—to get well and to move on. I forgave my attackers and all those who had hurt me (including my dad). And perhaps even more importantly, I forgave myself. I forgave myself for the guilt, shame and blame I harbored in connection with the sexual assaults and for the poor life choices I had made since then.

Lastly, I trusted myself and God. I stopped believing the negative chatter in my head—that I do not matter and that I am damaged goods. I stopped letting people talk me out of doing the things I wanted to do. I trusted and believed that my steps are divinely ordered and that where I was at that moment was where I was supposed to be. I trusted and believed that God would reveal the reasons when necessary.

On this note, I invite you to join me in a moment of self-reflection. Pray for the transformation and renewing of your mind. Forgive those who have caused you pain and anguish, but also forgive yourself for whatever part you feel you may have played in what has happened. Do not be afraid to trust God and to trust yourself. Everything you need to create your new and positive future is already inside of you. You may tap into it any time, simply by believing, deep down that you can.

. 8 .

MAKING IT HAPPEN

In Chapter 6 I shared how I answered the call to start Phynyx Ministries on June 10, 2011 while watching Steve Harvey and Tyrese Gibson on TBN. So what did I do next?

Nothing.

Weeks passed by and I did absolutely nothing. Fear had returned and my inner critic came along for the ride. The negative chatter in my head was deafening. And it stung.

Nobody wants to hear what you have to say. You don't know what you are talking about. You don't even know where to begin, so you may as well not. Who do you think you are, anyway? Nobody cares. You're no doctor, no counselor, no minister—you can't start a ministry. You don't have any formal training. How can you help anyone? You're just Lil' Neicy from Eager Street, YOU CAN'T DO THAT!!!

For weeks, I let fear and negativity rob me of the strength and purpose that God had given me to empower Survivors to break their silence and heal. And it was not only the fear that was crippling me. I genuinely did not know how to get started. All I knew was that I wanted to speak words of encouragement to Survivors in some way.

That summer, at a barbecue with Asia's godparents Tanya and Kil, I had the conversation that began to inch my plans forward. Tanya and I were eating in the kitchen and the guys were upstairs in Kil's music studio.

"Girl, you put a hurtin' on this tilapia," I said to Tanya, inhaling the delicious fish in between sentences. I was telling her that I had finally answered the call to start Phynyx Ministries, but could not seem to get started. I had shared the entire vision for the ministry with her a few years earlier and even then she thought I was crazy for not doing it.

"I wish I knew what my purpose was," Tanya said. "You know and you ain't doing nothing with it?"

I shared that perhaps I could start with a blog, which would allow me to speak life and encouragement into Survivors on a regular basis. I was about to digress when Tanya interrupted.

"Well, you know Kil is the blog king. Go on upstairs and ask him to help you."

"Naw girl, I'm not ready," I replied. "I can't."

In her loud, motherly voice, Tanya made it clear that this was not a suggestion.

"Take the tilapia and ya butt upstairs to get his help—he will hook you up."

And sure enough, Kil had my blog up in a matter of minutes. I could not believe it. Now, I thought, I was on my way!

Wrong again.

I was still so fearful, even of writing a simple blog post. I had so much in my head that I wanted to share, but I just could not bring myself to get it out. After days of agonizing over my first post, I threw caution to the wind. I felt the fear, but published it anyway.

The post was a photo of a young woman on the top of a mountain with her arms extended in victory and the scripture from Philippians 4:13, "I can do all things through Christ who strengthens me." This scripture has gotten me through so many difficult times—times at which I was met with enormous obstacles in an effort to complete tasks, projects or anything I felt was greater than me. It was a fitting start for what was to come.

After months of blogging, I felt it was time to move on to the next component of my vision for Phynyx Ministries and begin the church ministry. God told me that Phynyx Ministries must be in churches, but I must start at my home church first. I created and submitted a ministry proposal to my Pastor Rev. Dr. Jamal Harrison-Bryant, he approved it, and we kicked off Phynyx Ministries at the Empowerment Temple's Sexual Assault Healing Ministry (S.A.H.M.) on March 10, 2012.

We set the date for our first meeting a month later at the church's Family Life Center. My leadership team and I arrived to set up the room we had chosen with scented candles, boxes of Kleenex for those moments of overwhelm and chairs for about eight attendees. We had chosen the room (normally used as the youth game room) because it was warm and cozy and had a comforting feel to it, not to mention large plushy chairs. Truth be told, I was not expecting more than five women to actually show and my anxiety about the attendance grew the closer we got to starting time.

Finally, a young woman walked in and a huge, cheesy smile lit up my face. The heaviness of anticipated failure was lifted from my heart. I welcomed her to the meeting with a big hug as my team handed her a registration packet. As I turned around to gather my notes to begin the meeting, a few more women entered the room and before we could get them settled in, we had a very different challenge on our hands as more and more women showed up. We scrambled to add more chairs to the square of large plushy ones.

I was blown away by the influx of women that were seeking something that they so desperately needed, something to heal the pain of their experiences with sexual violence. A total of fifteen women attended our very first S.A.H.M. meeting. God had tripled my more modest expectations—little becomes much when you place it in the Master's hands. Not only did God show me that there is a tremendous need for this ministry, he also showed me what was on the other side of the fear.

Fear always shows up when there is something that you must do. The greater the fear, the greater the need for you to accomplish what lies before you. Courage is pushing past that fear and doing it anyway—taking action even when you feel afraid. As scripture tells us in 2 Timothy 1:7, "For God has not given us a spirit of fear, but of power, and of love, and of a sound mind." This helps us to understand that fear is just a distraction of the devil, created to throw us off of the road toward fulfilling our purposes. But every task we accomplish makes us more aware of our true strength and brings us yet another step closer to our destinies.

There were so many people waiting for me to step into my greatness so that they could be empowered and healed. I could not help but push past the fear and start Phynyx Ministries. And now, when I think about the hundreds of lives that have been impacted since its inception, I cannot help but thank and praise God for trusting Lil' Neicy from Eager Street with such a world changing purpose.

How might you step into your own greatness? Could it be that your pain holds the key to your purpose? Absolutely. God knew that He could trust you with the pain in order to birth purpose in you. There are people who need you and are waiting for you to make it happen.

. 9 .

DISCOVERING THE HOPE

As you come to the end of this book, I want you to understand that there is hope and it is available to you.

Perhaps surviving a sexual assault or another traumatic experience left you, like it did me, with a feeling that you will never be able to recover or heal. Over the many months following my second assault, I suffered from psychological maladies, including post-traumatic stress disorder. Severe stress and anxiety kept me locked in an imaginary prison from which I was afraid to escape. I felt no hope of ever picking up the pieces of my life and moving forward to a place of healing. And it is because I have experienced this psychological torture and overcome it that I can now tell you, with confidence:

> *Lift up your heads, O ye gates; and be ye lift up, ye everlasting doors; and the King of glory shall come in. Who is this King of glory? The LORD strong and mighty, the LORD mighty in battle.*

— Psalm 24:7-8

I know it was God who has not only saved me, but kept me even to this day, and He will do the same for you.

Psalm 121:7-8 tells us, "The LORD will keep you from all harm—he will watch over your life; the LORD will watch over your coming and going both now and forevermore." God has been with you and watching over you, as well. He knew you before you were even formed in your Mother's womb and already had plans for your life. And although you may have had one or many painful and or traumatic experiences, please understand that it was the grace and mercy of God that has kept you.

Perhaps you are blaming yourself, as I did. Maybe you are experiencing a severe case of the "if onlys."

If only I hadn't trusted this person...

If only I had screamed...

If only I hadn't gone up to his room...

If only I hadn't gone to that party...

If only hadn't worn that little black dress...

If only I hadn't invited him over for a nice home-cooked meal...

We Survivors often begin by blaming ourselves for a part we feel that we may have played in our assault. This is a form of victim thinking, and it is normal for victims to regret what they have done in the past and to wish things had been different. But please know that as Survivors of sexual assault, blaming ourselves is one of the most damaging things we can do. And the truth is that being sexually assaulted is never your fault.

Taking responsibility for what a perpetrator did is traumatizing all over again. We must remember, instead, that the decisions we made and the actions we took during the assault enabled us to survive it. We must value ourselves for making the best decisions we could at that time, decisions that very well may have saved our lives.

Even our loved ones can sometimes lose sight of the fact that while we are responsible for our own actions—we are not responsible for the actions of others. So it is ever more important to take a moment to say aloud:

The sexual violence that I have experienced was not my fault. I did nothing to cause it. I forgive myself, I honor myself and I know that I am empowered by my past. I will no longer settle in the place of darkness that has kept me from shining my light for all to see. From this day forward I will be hopeful and not hopeless. I am no longer a Victim, I am a Survivor!

You may be wondering, "How can I discover the hope?" You can start by praying and seeking God's guidance, changing your perspective, taking action, showing gratitude and learning when to seek help. Trust that taking these actions will bring the hope you seek and you will soon discover that your past does not define you. You can be in a healthy loving relationship. You can get married. You are deserving of love. You can have children. You can own a business. You can lead a ministry. You can change lives. You can heal. You can LIVE!

So when you feel hopeless and unloved, know that you are full of life and abundantly loved.

RESOURCES

Rape, Abuse & Incest National Network (RAINN)
2000 L Street, MW Suite 406
Washington, DC 20036
rainn.org

Rescued & Redeemed
(for advocacy and education on sex trafficking)
(888) 400-1571
info@rescuedredeemed.org
rescuedredeemed.org

Safe Horizon
(800) 621-HOPE
safehorizon.org

National Sexual Assault Hotline
(800) 656-HOPE (4673)

Speaking Out About Rape, Inc. (SOAR)
3208 Colonial Drive Unit 243
Orlando, FL 32803
(321) 278-5246
soar99.org

Stop It Now
(888) PREVENT
stopitnow.org

National Suicide Prevention Lifeline
(800) 273-TALK

Survivors of Incest Anonymous World Service Office
P.O. Box 190
Benson, MD 21018-9998
(410) 893-3322
siawso.org

National Suicide Crisis Hotline
(800) SUICIDE (784-2433)

Safer Campus
(for college students)
safercampus.org

Phynyx Ministries, Inc.
(443) 317-3070
phynyxministries.org

SURVIVOR AFFIRMATIONS

Please place this list of Survivor Affirmations in an area where you can review and recite daily to gain strength and be empowered to break through persistent obstacles and challenges the day may bring.

I am an innocent child of God.

God's light and love wash over me.

I open my heart to light and love.

My light shines more and more each day.

I am a pure being of light and love.

I let go of the past and embrace a future filled with light and love and hope.

I am empowered by my past; I'm a survivor.

I fully accept my past and acknowledge my resilience.

God's unconditional love for me is infinite.

My self-esteem increases with every breath I take.

God's love for me washes away my shame.
My soul is part of God and it is pure.

ABOUT THE AUTHOR

Angela D. Wharton, is an author, speaker and visionary founder of Phynyx Ministries, Inc., a Christian-based non-profit organization that provides a pathway to healing for women sexual assault survivors through love, support, service, empowerment and education. A woman of enormous faith and a two-time survivor of a sexual assault, Angela is a devoted wife and mother of two young girls on an unchartered mission of healing, wholeness, empowerment and love. Stepping out on faith to implement her God-given vision to establish Phynyx Ministries, Angela has been reassuring and strengthening survivors of sexual violence since 2011.

Her message of hope and healing has reached thousands through her partnerships with media, local churches, community organizations, advocacy groups, colleges and universities. Angela has hosted and spoken at workshops and numerous other events for wide ranging audiences including senior citizens, university students and faculty, faith communities, recovering substance abusers, and the public at large. Angela has twice served as a panelist at Morgan State University events, including the Male Forum Against Domestic Violence. She also testified before the State Judiciary Committee in support of legislation to make sex offenders' past history admissible in court.

Angela has made appearances on local radio and television in Baltimore, including WHUR's the Daily Drum, where the topic was the sexual harassment of women on the streets.

Angela is dedicated to providing survivors with hope in the face of hopelessness, courage in the presence of fear, strength to break the silence and the power to move to forgiveness – all with the ultimate goal for the survivor to recapture love, unconditionally and heal.

For more information, please visit us at:
PhynyxMinistries.org

I WANT TO HEAR FROM YOU!!!

If this book has made a difference in your life or in the life of someone you know, Angela would be delighted to hear about it. **Leave a review on Amazon.com!**

Book Angela to Speak at your event!

Send an email to angeladwharton@gmail.com
or visit her website:

www.AngelaDWharton.com

■ ■ ■

Follow me on social media

f /angela.d.wharton

🐦 @phynyxxskyy and @phynyxministrie